CRYPTO
FROM HILLS TO
HOLDINGS

Printed in (UNITED STATES)

First Printing edition 2023.

TABLE OF CONTENTS

CHAPTER ONE

THE TURNING POINTS

As I stepped through the door, the weariness from that relentless 12-hour hospital shift wasn't just in my muscles; it seemed to seep into my very bones. The exhaustion mirrored the strain of my financial worries, a weight I carried heavily as a single mother. The looming shadow of bankruptcy added to the burden, pressing down on me relentlessly. In those solitary moments, as evening settled and the dim light cast gloom over my modest home, I sank into the worn-out sofa. The weight of my concerns was palpable in the heavy silence enveloped me.

I used to see those pillows as plush and welcoming, but now, they hold traces of my tears, absorbed into the fabric night after night. Amid this overwhelming despair, a spark of resilience ignited within me. In those quiet moments, I planted a seed of determination—a commitment to break free from the suffocating grip of financial struggle and uncertainty.

When the world was asleep, and the clock crept past midnight, I found myself wide awake, delving into the intricacies of this new financial landscape. It wasn't just about securing a stable future anymore; it was a battle to regain control and resist surrendering to impossible circumstances.

Between the chaos of my demanding day job and the responsibilities of motherhood, my resolve to comprehend and invest in this emerging market only grew. Every penny was precious, every sacrifice of luxury or necessity a contribution to assemble a modest capital—a starting point to steer me away from the financial abyss.

Nestled within the serene yet challenging landscape of the Appalachian Mountains lay Hazard, a town once thriving with the pulse of coal mines that sustained its economy. However, as the coal industry dwindled, the once-vibrant community began to weather the storms of economic decline. Jobs became scarce, opportunities faded, and the town's resilience was tested.

In the heart of this town, I've always been rooted deep, feeling its pulse with every change that sweeps through.

But these recent shifts hit me harder than most. The closure of the mines snatched away the sturdy jobs we relied on, leaving us grasping at vanished opportunities. No matter how hard I tried, finding stable work became a dream, slipping further away. Our town's economy, once our foundation, now resembled a hollow shell haunted by missed chances.

Then came that certified letter, a brutal blow landing squarely on whatever stability I clung to. It threatened foreclosure on my modest home, tearing away my last shreds of security. In a place where everyone seemed entangled in financial woes, help and resources were as scarce as water in a drought. Even friends and neighbors, usually pillars of support, were wrestling with their hardships, unable to throw a lifeline. The weight of debt grew daily, burdening me with an unbearable heaviness.

Each dawn brought fresh uncertainty, and nights were restless with worry. Once familiar and comforting, Hazard now felt alien, almost hostile, draped in the shadow of economic hardship.

Yet, amidst this desolation, I stood, carrying my burdens and the weight of the town's decline. The foreclosure notice wasn't just about financial ruin—it was a jolting wake-up call. A challenge that pushed me to seek new paths, to defy the looming despair, and to find a way out of this bleak landscape.

Despite my dedication and hard work as a respiratory therapist at Appalachian Regional Healthcare, I faced a stark reality—my compensation wasn't commensurate with similar roles elsewhere in the state. This discrepancy in pay was a constant struggle, especially considering the cost of living in my area. Undeterred by the financial constraints, my determination to secure a better future propelled me to seek additional work opportunities.

With an unwavering resolve to improve my financial situation, I made the most of every available hour of overtime at the hospital pushing myself to the limit, maximizing the efforts to bridge the gap between earnings and the standard pay for my profession.

One particular day, as I navigated the familiar halls of the hospital, a glimmer of opportunity caught my eye—an unexpected chance for a different role. Posters advertising security jobs dotted the corridors. It was a moment that sparked contemplation within me—a juncture was considering the possibility of diversifying my skill set to supplement the income coming in.

The prospect of additional work outside my primary role as a respiratory therapist intrigued me. However, it also posed a dilemma. Would pursuing this opportunity demand more of my time and energy balancing my responsibilities at the hospital with a potential security position weighed heavily on my mind.

The demanding hours in healthcare required my undivided attention, yet the allure of a security role intrigued me. I pondered the feasibility of managing both worlds: the urgency of patient care and the vigilance needed in a security position. The prospect seemed daunting, but the challenge ignited a spark of determination within me. Finding an equilibrium between these roles would require careful planning and unwavering commitment.

In that pivotal moment, I was at a crossroads in my journey. It wasn't just about making ends meet; it was a testament to my determination to transcend the boundaries imposed by my circumstances. It symbolized my readiness to embrace unfamiliar paths, even if they initially seemed intimidating.

My journey started from modest beginnings. Standing outside the downtown office in Hazard, my heart pounded with nervous energy. The weight of my situation pressed down on me, and the urgency to secure employment hung heavy in the air.

Walking into the office, my nerves tingled as I confronted a stern-faced woman behind a cluttered desk. Tears welled as I poured out my story—details of the hardships I faced in Kentucky, the relentless pursuit of financial stability, and the burning passion to break free from fate's constraints.

To my surprise, instead of a dismissive gesture or a polite refusal, the lady listened intently. Her eyes showed a glimmer of understanding and a rare empathy for the unwavering determination that fueled me. In that moment of vulnerability, I bared my soul, sharing my aspirations and fears without reservation.

I stood there, my breath caught in my throat as the lady across from me paused, seemingly lost in thought. It felt like an eternity before she extended a hand, offering me a tissue. A glimmer of hope ignited within me at that moment as her expression softened.

I can't promise much," she began, her voice a blend of compassion and authority, "but I believe in giving chances to those who fight for them. We're short-handed. Can you start tomorrow?

My heart raced, and a whirlwind of emotions flooded me—gratitude, relief, and a newfound determination. Though the offered wage of $7.25 an hour might seem meager to some, to me, it was an opportunity—an opportunity to start forging my path to a better future.

The following day, I walked through the office doors, a mix of nerves and excitement swirling in my stomach. The air seemed charged with the scent of new beginnings as I sat at the desk. Each keystroke and phone call felt like markers of the start of my ascent—a humble yet relentless climb from the depths of uncertainty toward a brighter horizon.

The reality of being the only woman in a male-dominated workplace was a daily trial. Assigned tasks seemed carefully selected to match their aversion rather than my skills. Mere glances and subtle smirks conveyed what their words didn't dare. Some of my colleagues made jest of my presence right to my face while the whispers and stifled laughs behind my back echoed in the corridors.

I could have let their mockery sting and carve insecurities into my determination, but I had a grander vision. Each shift from the respiratory unit to security reminded me of my resilience. Those hours weren't just ticking seconds; they were valuable coupons I meticulously collected for a better future.

The exhaustion wasn't just physical but a relentless tug on my spirit. Nights blurred into days, and fatigue became a companion I couldn't shake off. I wasn't fresh out of school or new to life's challenges. As they say, I was no spring chicken, but I was far from done with spreading my wings and soaring.

I stood there, burdened by the weight of the pounds that clung to my body and the heaviness of life's challenges that seemed impossible. It was in my late 40s when I made a decision—a pivotal moment that would change the course of my life. With a determined resolve, I headed to a local weight loss clinic.

The clinic seemed like any other ordinary place, a hub of hopes and aspirations for those seeking transformation. Little did I know that this visit would become a turning point for my physical health and the trajectory of my entire existence.

As I sat in the waiting room, clad in my security uniform, a doctor caught sight of me. There was something in her gaze, a curiosity that transcended the routine interactions she had with patients. She approached me in a moment that felt serendipitous, breaking the silence with a simple yet profound question: What's your story?

Caught off guard, I found myself pouring out my life's narrative in a mere ten minutes. I spoke of struggles, perseverance, and dreams that seemed distant amid life's relentless demands. My voice quivered with the weight of unspoken emotions, and tears welled up, betraying the stoic facade I'd worn for years.

To my surprise, her response wasn't just empathetic words or fleeting sympathy. Instead, it was an unexpected job opportunity that resonated with promise and possibility. It was an invitation to step into a new realm and rewrite my future.

This job wasn't just about the paycheck, though it promised financial relief akin to my primary source of income. It was about elevation—both in status and spirit. It marked the inception of a new journey, one where I would not just shed physical weight but also the burdens of my past.

With hesitant yet hopeful steps, I embarked on this uncharted path, unsure of where it would lead but resolute in my determination to seize this chance for change. Little did I know that this encounter would serve as a prelude to an even grander adventure, a tale woven with resilience, courage, and unexpected opportunities.

Working at the hospital wasn't just a job for me—it was a testament to my determination. The long shifts and countless hours blurred into a continuous stream of commitment. I pushed myself beyond limits, embracing every available moment to earn. Nights at the hospital merged seamlessly into days at the clinic, a whirlwind of activity that left no room for breaks or even a quick meal. The clinic, bustling with patients, became my second home. Alongside two other women on the brink of retirement, our reasons for being there might have differed, but our shared urgency was palpable.

In those intense moments, we forged a bond through our shared dedication. Our lives intersected in this rush, driven by financial goals but bound together by the sheer determination to make every moment count. Whether to secure a future, fulfill dreams, or survive the crunch time, we were united in pursuing something more.

The fatigue was relentless, but so was my resolve. The rhythm of relentless work became a part of me, shaping my understanding of perseverance and resilience. It wasn't just about the hours—it was about pushing past the exhaustion, finding strength in the most demanding hours, and realizing that sometimes, the most challenging moments lay the groundwork for the most remarkable transformations.

In the clinic, amid the sometimes harsh and even verbally abusive demeanor of the doctor, there was an unexpected silver lining. It was an unconventional classroom where finance wasn't just discussed, it was an unfiltered education that I, coming from a financially strained background in the 80s, had never experienced before. Money was a taboo subject in our household that often lingered in the shadows. Yet, here I was, absorbing invaluable lessons amidst the chaos of medical practices.

My upbringing, entrenched in poverty, shaped my aspirations. I was determined that my sons wouldn't witness the same struggles. I became a fervent advocate for education as the key to unlocking the shackles of our small-town existence, a place that, in my eyes, felt like an emotional prison—a confinement from broader opportunities and possibilities.

Like a mantra to my sons, I repeated, you'll go to school, and you'll leave this place. It wasn't just about physical departure but about liberating their minds, exposing them to the vast world beyond our limited horizons. The clinic, with its tough lessons and abrasive atmosphere, inadvertently fueled my resolve to break free from financial constraints and offer my sons a different narrative—a future unbound by the limitations I had faced.

After several months of working tirelessly at the clinic, our boss occasionally surprised us with bonuses. It was a welcomed relief after days packed with patient consultations. I'd often tell myself these bonuses were for survival, but truth be told, every once in a while, I'd indulge, treating myself to a decent meal or picking up something special for my sons. Little rewards for the endless hours of hard work.

But then came the day when our boss called us together for a meeting. She had this way of referring to us as 'girls,' despite us being grown women. It was a peculiar habit that always managed to amuse and irritate me at the same time. As the last patient filed out and the clinic quieted down, she dropped the bombshell—'We're forming a millionaires club,' she announced. Our collective reaction was a mix of surprise, skepticism, and a hint of disbelief. I remember exchanging glances with my colleagues, each expression echoing my inner thoughts: 'This is unreal, isn't it?

The notion of a 'millionaires club' seemed far-fetched in our reality. It was one of those moments where you couldn't help but stifle a laugh at the sheer audacity of the suggestion. I couldn't help but think, 'Is this some sort of joke?' But our boss, with a deadpan expression that indicated she was absolutely serious, continued on, outlining what seemed like an improbable plan.

Being part of the Millionaires Club was like entering a realm of financial revelations. My coworkers and I found ourselves in a room where our financial struggles were laid bare, and our past missteps faced scrutiny. Often, we were on the receiving end of raised eyebrows and silent judgments, especially when disclosing our predicament of living paycheck to paycheck. It felt like a stark contrast to the seemingly effortless financial stability of those around us.

At first, it was hard to fathom how someone who seemed to swim in wealth could genuinely empathize with the daily grind of making ends meet. There was a divide, a chasm between our realities. Yet, looking back, it's possible that the boss did understand—perhaps it was a phase in their life when the toil bore fruit, and they reaped the rewards of their hard work.

Our boss, an unexpected beacon in our financial storm, introduced us to a novel concept—the "snowball method." It was an unconventional approach, first paying off the smallest debts and progressing to the larger ones. Initially, it sounded peculiar and garnered skeptical glances from us. We'd often share furtive eye rolls behind the boss's back, hoping our doubts wouldn't be noticed.

But as we began implementing this method, gradual progress surfaced. Doubt turned into curiosity, and skepticism transformed into a newfound hope. It was a slow climb, but the boss's teachings started to resonate. Their patience in the face of our initial resistance was admirable.

Then, there was the vision board—a canvas for our dreams and aspirations. Crafting our aspirations on poster boards became a ritual, a tangible reminder of what lay ahead. Our weekly meetings evolved from mere discussions to sanctuaries where we shared dreams, assessed progress, and devised strategies for our financial breakthroughs.

Bonuses, usually fleeting moments of happiness for many, took on a different meaning for us. Instead of instant gratification, they became tools to chip away at our debts. Adjusting our perspective on bonuses was a process, a shift from short-term relief to long-term gains.

The boss's guidance initially met with doubt, became the cornerstone of our transformation. Their lessons transcended finances; they were about resilience, patience, and the power of envisioning a brighter future.

Cryptocurrency was an enigma—an uncharted realm promising uncertainty and limitless potential. Late nights turned into early mornings as I devoured information, attempting to decipher the complexities of blockchain technology and digital assets. It was like learning a new language, each concept unlocking a door to a world teeming with possibilities.

CHAPTER TWO

THE LEAP OF FAITH

Amid a rather sad afternoon, an article caught my eye—a piece that would change the trajectory of my financial journey. It was a piece on cryptocurrency, a term buzzing with excitement and intrigue. Curious, I brought up this newfound fascination at our next millionaire's club gathering. It was the year 2017, a time marked by a genuine bull market in the world of finance.

The air crackled with anticipation as I delved into the topic. Cryptocurrency wasn't just a passing trend but a paradigm shifts in the financial landscape. Conversations hummed with excitement, echoing the enthusiasm of a market on the brink of a revolution.

As I discussed the hype surrounding this digital currency phenomenon, I felt a rush of curiosity mingled with a hint of skepticism. Yet, there was an undeniable allure to this uncharted territory. The allure of a potential opportunity, a chance to navigate uncharted waters and, perhaps, discover a new path to financial prosperity.

Little did I know that seemingly ordinary discussion would sow the seeds of a profound journey that would test my limits, challenge my perceptions, and ultimately redefine my understanding of risk and reward in finance.

Every morning, our boss would hand out assignments as though she held the keys to our livelihoods. The pressure was palpable; it was clear that failing to meet her demands meant facing a storm of consequences. She didn't just expect results; she demanded them, with an unspoken threat lingering in the air - our jobs were on the line.

There were times when the threat of termination hovered over us like a dark cloud. The mere suggestion that we might think ourselves worthy of our wages was met with a stern warning, reminding us of her power over our livelihoods. It wasn't just about the work; it was about survival.

The tension escalated when she wielded the ultimate control—our paychecks. At her whim, she would withhold our hard-earned money, a tactic that sent a clear message: comply or suffer the consequences. It was a coercive dance where fear choreographed every move.

We knew, without a doubt, that our only option was to toe the line, adhere to her every demand, and execute the tasks she set before us. The price of defiance wasn't just uncertainty but the potential loss of everything we had worked for.

In that high-stakes environment, each assignment became a battle to prove our worth, not just for the work but for our stability. The fear she instilled in us was the fuel that kept us obedient, even if it meant sacrificing our peace of mind.

The workplace atmosphere crackled with tension and fear, a constant reminder that our fates were not entirely in our own hands. But amid this pressure cooker of demands and threats, a seed of defiance and a dream for something better quietly took root within me."

The allure of cryptocurrency pulled us into an exhilarating new world that demanded a complete overhaul of our understanding. It began with a thirst for knowledge, a hunger to decipher the enigmatic language of digital assets that seemed light years away from our country's roots.

As we embarked on this path, the first step was education. It wasn't just about grasping the concepts; it was a quest to untangle the web of terminology that seemed foreign and complex. Blockchain, mining, wallets—terms echoed through forums and articles, leaving us grappling to comprehend their significance. Our minds, so accustomed to the tangible, struggled to grasp the intangible nature of these assets.

Yet, our curiosity was insatiable. We poured over guides, devoured articles, and engaged in countless discussions, each word a stepping stone toward unraveling this technological marvel. Every concept learned felt like a victory over the initial bewilderment that had clouded our understanding.

Picture two eager minds, fueled by curiosity, spending nights delving into the fundamentals of crypto. It wasn't just about the profit potential; it was about breaking through the barriers of our limited understanding, transcending the geographical confines that once seemed like impenetrable barriers to this digital universe.

As we gradually absorbed the basics, we marveled at the intricate design of this financial frontier. The sheer magnitude of this shift from tangible cash to virtual currencies became more apparent with each passing day. It wasn't just about money; it was a paradigm shift, a redefinition of wealth and value transcending physical boundaries.

And amidst this whirlwind of learning, there was an undeniable thrill—the rush that comes with venturing into the unknown. It wasn't just about the challenge of understanding; it was about embracing the transformation, allowing ourselves to be swept away by the momentum of a technological revolution.

Our journey into the world of crypto was just beginning, and every stumbling block was an opportunity to deepen our understanding and bridge the gap between our country's roots and the digital realm that promised so much potential.

The cryptocurrency journey was an odyssey marked by a maze of unfamiliar terms and concepts, a lexicon that felt like an encrypted language only the initiated could comprehend. It was like stepping foot into a bustling city where everyone spoke a dialect foreign to our ears.

The very foundation of this adventure lay in understanding the bedrock—the terminology. Words like "blockchain" and "decentralization" echoed in our minds, initially sounding like jargon from a different universe. We found ourselves immersed in a sea of acronyms—BTC, ETH, ICO, HODL—each holding a key to a different facet of this enigmatic landscape.

The very notion of digital assets, intangible yet possessing immense value, was a concept that defied the logic of our upbringing. In our small-town existence, money meant physical bills and coins securely nestled in a tangible wallet. The idea of a virtual wallet, a repository for digital wealth, seemed more like a figment of a sci-fi novel than a practical financial concept.

As we stepped into the crypto-verse, it was like wandering uncharted land. The thrill of exploration fueled our quest for understanding, pushing us to devour every resource available. Articles, videos, forums—our days turned into a crash course in a language that felt alien yet held the key to a new financial frontier.

As we plunged into the basics, we realized the cornerstone of this financial revolution lay in the blockchain—a decentralized ledger that underpinned the entire crypto world. The beauty of this technology lies in its transparency, a shared database across a network of computers, safeguarding each transaction with cryptographic security.

Mining, a term that conjured images of hardhats and pickaxes in our rural minds, took on a completely different meaning. It wasn't about extracting precious metals from the earth; instead, it was validating and recording transactions on the blockchain, rewarded with newly minted digital currencies.

Wallets, not the leather ones we used to carry, transformed into digital vaults safeguarding our cryptographic keys—keys that unlocked access to our digital fortunes. ICOs (Initial Coin Offerings), akin to IPOs in the traditional financial world, were our introduction to new digital currencies, their launches marked with both excitement and caution.

In those early days, the glossary of terms felt overwhelming, a complex tapestry that needed decoding. Yet, with each passing day, each article read, and every conversation engaged in, the fog lifted bit by bit. Concepts that initially seemed esoteric gradually became comprehensible, and we began piecing together the mosaic of knowledge that formed the foundation of our journey.

Wrapped in the allure of this technological marvel, we were drawn to the fundamental concept—the blockchain.

The decentralized ledger became our compass, guiding us through a landscape where transactions were secure, transparent, and beyond the control of a single entity.

Then came the initiation—acquiring our first digital asset. It wasn't just a transaction but a rite of passage, a tangible link to this virtual universe. Navigating exchanges and understanding the dynamics of buying and selling—each step felt like planting a flag in this uncharted territory.

Yet, with each triumph came the realization of volatility. The rollercoaster nature of the market greeted us with exhilarating highs and heart-stopping lows. The risks loomed large, teaching us that fortunes could shift in a heartbeat in this realm.

But it wasn't a solitary journey. Engaging with the vibrant crypto community became our sanctuary. Online forums and social media groups became havens of shared experiences and knowledge. Discussions weren't just about the market; they were windows into a community bonded by a shared passion.

Beyond the financial gains lay a more profound transformation. It was a paradigm shift—a rewiring of our perceptions about money and value. The journey as beginners wasn't just about decoding terminology or understanding the market; it was an embrace of a new way of envisioning wealth—a decentralized digital landscape that promised risks and boundless possibilities.

The first steps into the world of crypto were more than a learning curve; they were an initiation into a realm where curiosity, determination, and a willingness to adapt were the currencies of survival. It was the beginning of an odyssey that promised both challenges and the potential for remarkable discovery.

Understanding the fundamentals became paramount. It wasn't merely about investing but deciphering the ebbs and flows of this digital realm. Bull markets and bear markets weren't just terms; they were the heartbeat of an entire ecosystem. Learning to distinguish between them was like deciphering a code that could unlock or lock away potential fortunes.

The concept of a bear market, where pessimism dominated, and prices plummeted, stood in stark contrast to the enthusiasm of a bull market, where optimism soared, and values surged. These weren't just fluctuations on a screen; they were indicators of an entire ecosystem's mood that dictated strategies and tested nerves.

And in this swirling sea of information, we began to grasp the essence of this unconventional market—a place not just for the financially adept but for those willing to immerse themselves in a new way of thinking, navigating through uncertainty with knowledge as their compass. The allure was magnetic, but the learning curve was steep. Yet, it was precisely this challenge that kindled an unyielding determination within us.

As I delved deeper into cryptocurrencies, it was like stepping into a labyrinthine treasure trove of digital assets. At the forefront stood Bitcoin, the OG of the crypto realm—a revolutionary concept that had transformed how we perceived money. Its meteoric rise in 2017, soaring to an unprecedented $20,000, made headlines and set the stage for a frenzy of digital currency exploration.

But Bitcoin was just the tip of the iceberg. Altcoins— Ether, XRP, Litecoin, and many others—each had its tale to tell. Ethereum, not merely a digital currency but a platform enabling decentralized applications through smart contracts, captivated me with its potential to revolutionize industries beyond finance.

The allure of Ripple, designed to streamline cross-border payments, spoke volumes about the practical applications of cryptocurrencies in the financial world. Litecoin, often dubbed the silver to Bitcoin's gold, caught my attention with its faster transaction times and lower fees, paving the way for experimentation and innovation within the crypto space.

Then newer contenders like Cardano and Polkadot emerged, each with a distinct vision and technological edge. Cardano's meticulous approach, grounded in academic research, promised a more secure and scalable blockchain. In contrast, Polkadot's emphasis on blockchain interoperability hinted at a future where digital assets could seamlessly communicate and transact.

Navigating these digital currencies was akin to exploring a vast, uncharted territory. Each coin had unique features, strengths, and communities rallying behind it. Yet, the volatility of this nascent market was palpable, swinging between ecstatic highs and nerve-racking downturns, teaching me the ropes of this exhilarating yet unpredictable landscape.

The YouTube gurus became my guides through this maze, offering insights and cautionary tales and deciphering the complexities of charts and trends. Every video was a window into the potential and pitfalls of this new frontier—a digital Wild West where fortunes were made and lost with the rise and fall of the sun.

The world of cryptocurrencies was not just about numbers; it was an evolving saga of technological prowess, financial revolution, and the perpetual quest for understanding the future hidden within lines of code and digital currencies.

The allure of these altcoins was magnetic, each presenting its unique utility and potential. However, the volatility was a rollercoaster ride I couldn't have prepared for. One day, the charts gleamed with vibrant green, promising a future brimming with possibilities, only for the next day to plunge into a sea of red, leaving heads spinning and hearts racing.

It was like navigating through a digital storm—each coin, a vessel with its sails catching winds of speculation and market sentiment. The excitement was palpable, but so was the unpredictability. The YouTube gurus spun tales of fortunes made overnight and cautioned against the explosive nature of this financial Wild West. Amidst the euphoria of potential gains, the reality of abrupt downturns loomed large, teaching me the harsh lessons of a market that danced between exhilarating highs and nerve-wracking lows.

The allure of these coins was not just their financial promise but the underlying technologies—the blockchain, smart contracts, and the potential to revolutionize industries. Yet, in the blink of an eye, the market mood swung, dictating the fate of fortunes and investments. This volatility became the heartbeat of an industry that never slept, an ecosystem where fortunes were made and lost with the rise and fall of the sun.

In this ever-shifting landscape, deciphering the patterns, understanding the trends, and distinguishing between the hype and the substance became an art I yearned to master. Each YouTube video was a puzzle piece, an insight into this enigmatic realm where one day's expert advice could become the next day's cautionary tale.

It was a wild ride, navigating through this maze of coins and currencies, where every rise and fall held a lesson, and every dip was an opportunity in disguise. The world of cryptocurrencies wasn't just about numbers—it was a relentless, thrilling saga of hope, risk, and the perpetual quest for understanding the future hidden within lines of code and digital currencies.

The Millionaires Club's decision to take that leap of faith felt like a wild dive into the unknown. Picture this: a bunch of us, each with the enthusiasm to succeed but collectively resembling the blind leading the blind. At times, it teetered on the edge of comical until the gravity of our hard-earned money hung in the balance.

Our boss, a powerhouse of determination, led us zealously. She'd hand out assignments and, like clockwork, verbally quiz us the very next working day. As a grown woman, finding myself under the control of another, even if she was a grown woman herself, grated against my independence. It felt like dancing to someone else's tune when I longed for the rhythm of my life.

Yet, within this controlled chaos, seeds of opportunity were sown. The frustration of being directed like a marionette pushed me to evaluate what I sought in my career. It ignited a fire within, a burning desire to craft my path, to take the reins and steer my destiny.

Sure, it was exasperating at times, feeling like I was in a perpetual game where the rules were ever-shifting. But in hindsight, it was within this apparent chaos that the first sparks of my journey towards financial freedom were kindled. The discomfort and the sense of constraint all contributed to the awakening of a determination that would one day drive me toward unforeseen success.

The Millionaire's Club was our starting point—a curious blend of frustration, camaraderie, and a hint of absurdity. Little did we know that the humble beginnings of an adventure would redefine our understanding of control, success, and the true power of autonomy.

The first step on our crypto journey was finding the proper exchange—a digital gateway to the thrilling world of cryptocurrencies. After much research and contemplation, we settled on Coinbase. Creating an account felt like stepping into uncharted territory, a realm buzzing with potential and uncertainty.

Donna and I exchanged glances, laughter bubbling up as we hovered over the 'Sign Up' button. The thrill of embarking on this financial adventure was tinged with a hint of nervousness. Verifying our identities and linking our bank accounts brought a momentary pause; a fleeting thought crossed my mind: What if we're in over our heads?

The familiar ding of email notifications broke the silence, guiding us through the validation process. As I filled in my details, I couldn't help but wonder about the potential outcomes of this new endeavor. Would this leap of faith lead to financial liberation or teach us a costly lesson?

We don't even have any spare change in those accounts, Donna teased, her laughter echoing the sentiments I couldn't quite say. We were indeed stepping into this with empty pockets and hearts full of curiosity. But sometimes, it's not about the amount you start with; it's about the journey and the knowledge gained along the way.

With a click, our accounts were created, beginning our thrilling expedition into cryptocurrency's volatile yet exhilarating world.

Imagine this: May 22, 2010, a date etched into the history of cryptocurrencies. With infectious enthusiasm, our boss recounted the tale of Laszlo Hanyecz, an innovator ahead of his time. He did something seemingly mundane yet groundbreaking. He bought not just one but two Papa John's pizzas from Jeremy Sturdivant, paying a humble

10,000 Bitcoins for the cheesy delight. It was a transaction—two pizzas for a bunch of digital coins. Little did anyone grasp the seismic value this seemingly simple exchange would hold.

Fast forward to 2017, the year of jaw-dropping realizations. That same stash of 10,000 Bitcoins, back when they were a mere experimental currency, would've skyrocketed into a mind-bending fortune of $200,000,000. It was the inception of Bitcoin's real-world use, a spark that ignited a firestorm of possibilities.

Our boss, an oracle of wisdom in cryptocurrencies, would fervently emphasize the power of patience. 'Hold onto your coins,' she'd emphasize, her voice carrying the weight of experience. 'The real gains come with time. It's not about the instant thrill; it's about the marathon.'

She'd paint a vivid picture, urging us to think beyond the momentary allure of quick profits. 'It's the long game,' she'd say, her eyes gleaming with the tales of those who dared to wait, to hold onto their digital treasures as they grew from experimental curiosities to transformative assets.

As I absorbed her words, I couldn't help but ponder the immense power hidden within those virtual coins. The notion of holding onto something so intangible, so volatile yet potentially life-altering, resonated deeply. It wasn't just about currencies; it was about trust, belief, and the unwavering commitment to a future that was yet to reveal its promise fully.

That story of the pizza transaction once brushed off as a quirky anecdote, became a beacon—a testament to the incredible journey that cryptocurrencies were embarking upon. It wasn't just about pizzas; it was about rewriting the rules of value, reshaping our perceptions of wealth, and challenging the conventional with the boundless possibilities of the digital age."

Entering the world of cryptocurrency felt like stepping into the unknown—a terrain painted by ominous myths and cautionary tales. The air was thick with skepticism, fueled by whispers of bitcoins being a tool for the unseen, a realm where only the tech-savvy dared to tread. We were trapped by the prevailing notion that this space was a breeding ground for criminals, a playground of anonymity where illegal activities thrived unchecked. It was easy to succumb to the belief that this was a scam lurking in the shadows, waiting to pounce on the naive.

The fear was palpable; each step forward seemed shrouded in uncertainty. Misinformation circulated like wildfire, and every mention of cryptocurrencies added another layer of doubt. We questioned if we were being lured into a trap, led astray by a mirage promising riches but concealing peril.

But amidst this trepidation, a flicker of curiosity burned within. What if these notions were just one side of the story? What if, beyond the veil of fear, lay a world of potential and opportunity? This curiosity nudged us to take that first tentative step, to look beyond the myths and explore the truth for ourselves.

With cautious optimism, determination, and an insatiable thirst for knowledge, we began to unravel the mysteries of this enigmatic world. We sought credible sources and delved into the core principles of cryptocurrency, and slowly, the fog of misconceptions began to lift.

As the layers of misinformation peeled away, we discovered that beneath the murky rumors lay a technology that held transformative potential. The same features rumored to attract criminal elements—decentralization, security, and anonymity—also promised a revolutionary way of conducting transactions and building trust.

The journey was not without its doubts and hesitations. The shadow of those initial myths lingered, but our persistence outweighed the fear. We unearthed not a scam reserved for the select few but a frontier where the bold and determined could carve their paths, a realm that rewarded knowledge, strategy, and foresight.

The evolution from fear to fascination was a testament to the power of exploring beyond preconceived notions. It was a journey that taught us that sometimes, the most daunting landscapes held the wealthiest treasures, waiting for those daring enough to embark on the adventure.

Embarking on this venture was akin to stepping into uncharted territory, a journey of uncertainty and hope. As we set up our accounts, the thrill of diving into the cryptocurrency market filled us with a blend of anticipation and curiosity. Among the array of digital coins beckoning us, Ethos stood out—an intriguing prospect touted by a persuasive YouTuber. Their fervent predictions painted a portrait of exponential growth, promising a leap from mere cents to coveted dollars in a blink.

With each penny I could spare, I eagerly invested more into Ethos. The allure of potential prosperity fueled my every decision. I vividly recall the average price hovering around 50 cents—an entry point I deemed favorable, a threshold promising immense possibilities. The allure of these altcoins, these smaller tokens beyond the towering value of Bitcoin at that time, was irresistible. They felt within reach, more tangible, and potentially more rewarding, albeit accompanied by their inherent risks.

The prospect of owning a whole Bitcoin, valued then at a staggering $20,000, seemed daunting and out of reach. Instead, with their modest yet promising values, these altcoins held an allure that resonated deeply. It felt like being part of a movement, a grassroots community rooted in the belief that even the most minor investment could yield substantial returns.

As we amassed more of these altcoins, particularly Ethos, it wasn't merely a financial endeavor but a venture woven with a sense of empowerment and optimism. Each purchase felt like stitching a patchwork quilt of possibilities, weaving together aspirations for financial growth in an unpredictable yet thrilling landscape.

Ah, the golden rule of the crypto game—' buy when there's blood in the streets.' It's a cryptic way of saying that when the market plunges, that's often the best time to buy. Picture this: the prices drop, panic ensues, but seasoned investors see it as a clearance sale on coins. An opportunity, if you will, to snag digital treasures at bargain prices.

Learning the ins and outs of this exhilarating world wasn't just about buying and selling. It was a crash course in navigating a digital universe that speaks its language. We mastered the art of purchasing, transferring, and receiving various currencies, swiftly converting them to maximize our investments. Our vision boards weren't just filled with dreams; they were visual maps of our financial aspirations. We'd jot down our potential holdings, sketching scenarios where patience would be our greatest ally.

The process was both surreal and educational. Watching those numbers fluctuate on websites like CoinMarketCap wasn't just about monitoring investments; it was witnessing the ebb and flow of a dynamic ecosystem. It felt like part of an intricate puzzle, deciphering patterns and projecting what those digital coins could potentially blossom into if nurtured over time. It was an education unlike any other, though at times, it felt like chasing a dream that might forever stay just out of reach.

But there was an allure in this uncertainty, a thrill that came with every calculated risk. It was a rollercoaster of emotions—excitement, uncertainty, and a hint of disbelief that these virtual tokens could hold much weight in the real world. Yet, amid this digital whirlwind, lessons were etched into my being, shaping me into a navigator of this mesmerizing, ever-evolving landscape.

The decision to enter the crypto world was akin to stepping into a dense forest without a clear path. It was daunting, exhilarating, and riddled with questions. Did I have the financial prowess? Was I equipped with the proper knowledge? But amidst the doubts, one thing remained constant—my unwavering determination.

Utilizing every penny saved from those overtime shifts, I took my first tentative steps into this digital realm. It wasn't a substantial investment but a leap of faith, a statement of intent. The risks were palpable, the uncertainty a constant companion, yet embracing the unknown was an electric thrill.

HOW CRYPTO WORKS

In a world where traditional currencies have always been the norm, a new digital marvel emerged, creating waves that rippled across the financial landscape—cryptocurrency.

Picture a decentralized realm where no single authority holds dominion. Instead, an intricate network of computers collaborates to maintain the integrity of this digital currency. It all begins with blockchain, the backbone of crypto.

Imagine a chain of blocks, each securely linked to the next, containing a record of transactions. This ledger isn't stored in one place but duplicated across countless computers worldwide, making it tamper-resistant. Whenever a transaction occurs, it's bundled into a block, time-stamped, and added to the chain.

Now, this is where the miners come into play. These tech-savvy individuals harness the power of their computers to validate transactions. They compete to solve complex mathematical puzzles, aiming to be the first to verify and add a new block to the chain.

Once a miner solves the puzzle and adds a block, it's verified across the network. This consensus mechanism ensures agreement among all participants, preventing double-spending and fraud.

But what incentivizes these miners? Rewards! They receive a portion of the cryptocurrency for their efforts, encouraging them to continue contributing their computational power to the network.

Here's the twist—cryptocurrency isn't physical; it's purely digital. Its value isn't tied to any government or central bank but is determined by market demand and scarcity. For instance, Bitcoin has a finite supply capped at 21 million coins, which drives its value based on supply and demand dynamics.

Now, you might wonder about security. The cryptographic keys play a pivotal role. Each user has a public address (like an account number) and a private key (a digital signature) that grants access and ownership. Keeping the private key secure is paramount; losing it could mean losing access to your cryptocurrency forever.

As this digital saga unfolds, more cryptocurrencies beyond Bitcoin emerge, each with unique features and purposes. Some prioritize privacy, while others focus on scalability or intelligent contracts—self-executing contracts with the terms directly written into code.

Crypto's impact extends beyond finance. Its underlying technology, blockchain, finds applications in various industries, from supply chain management to voting systems, revolutionizing how data is stored and shared.

In this captivating narrative, the world of cryptocurrency emerges as a decentralized, transparent, and innovative ecosystem challenging the status quo of traditional finance, paving the way for a new era of digital transactions and possibilities.

CHAPTER THREE

WEATHERING THE STORM

The crypto market was a turbulent sea—ever-shifting, unpredictable, and demanding. It wasn't just about investing; it was about understanding the nuances, the subtle fluctuations that could turn tides in seconds.

Days turned into weeks, weeks into months, as I maneuvered through this labyrinth of investments. Research became my ally, and strategic decisions became my armor. There were moments of triumph—small victories that fueled my determination—and moments of doubt when the market's volatility rattled my confidence.

Navigating the unpredictable terrain of the crypto market was akin to traversing uncharted territory. Each day brought a rollercoaster of emotions—exhilaration and, at times, gut-wrenching defeat. In those moments of steep learning curves, the lessons etched themselves into our journey, engraving themselves as invaluable principles of patience, resilience, and the art of risk-taking.

The exhilaration was akin to a surge of adrenaline coursing through our veins, especially during those monumental wins that felt like conquering the summit of a formidable peak. It was the high of making strategic moves, witnessing the numbers climb, and feeling the rush of success. Yet, within those victories lay the shadows of defeat, moments where the market's volatility taught us hard lessons.

Patience became our unwavering companion, the silent force guiding our decisions. In the crypto realm, instant gratification was a mirage, and every successful venture demanded patience—waiting for the right moment to strike, invest, hold, or step back.

Resilience became our armor against the tide of uncertainty. We found the strength to rise again for every setback, dusting off doubts and forging ahead. The crypto landscape was an unforgiving teacher but also cultivated a spirit that refused to succumb to the storms.

And then there were the risks—the lifeblood of the crypto world. It wasn't just about tossing the dice but about calculated risks, understanding the trends, and embracing the unknown with measured confidence. It meant acknowledging that failure was a part of the journey, a stepping stone to eventual success.

In this dance between triumph and stumble, we discovered the essence of growth. The lessons weren't just about navigating numbers but about understanding ourselves—our thresholds for uncertainty, our capacity for resilience, and our determination to weather the storms that echoed the sentiments of the volatile market.

Amid the exhilarating crypto boom of 2017, the market's meteoric rise seemed unstoppable. Digital currencies soared to unprecedented heights, promising wealth and success to those who dared to invest. I was among those captivated by this frenzy, drawn in by the allure of quick gains and the promise of a brighter financial future.

THE RISE AND FALL OF CRYPTO

In the vibrant world of cryptocurrencies, the rise and fall of digital assets unfolds like an ever-shifting tale, woven with intrigue, passion, and unforeseen twists—a narrative governed not just by financial metrics but by a delicate dance of human emotions, innovation, and the winds of change.

Picture this: a bustling market square, bustling with chatter and anticipation. Whispers of a revolutionary technology—blockchain—ripple through the crowd. It's a concept shrouded in mystery, yet its potential to redefine finance and beyond hangs like an intoxicating promise.

In this intricate tapestry of possibilities, the rise of cryptocurrencies begins. It's not just about numbers on screens; it's about a collective dream that transcends borders, challenging traditional financial paradigms. The first whispers of Bitcoin echo through forums and discussions, sparking curiosity and planting the seeds of a digital revolution.

As the momentum gathers, the market becomes a stage where sentiments sway like a pendulum. News of technological breakthroughs sends ripples of optimism, propelling prices skyward. The media adds fuel to the fire—headlines touting miraculous gains, stories of overnight millionaires, and visions of a decentralized future captivate minds.

But in this saga of ascent, there's a shadow lurking—the uncertainty. Regulations cast an ominous hue, sometimes looming as a specter, other times fading into whispers. Governments grapple with understanding, attempting to tame this enigmatic force, injecting uncertainty into an otherwise vigorous narrative.

And so, the pendulum swings—fear and exhilaration in an intricate dance. Whales, silent giants in this digital ocean, maneuver the currents, orchestrating waves of euphoria and trepidation with calculated moves. Their whispers and actions reverberate, shaping the market's undulating landscape.

But amidst the chaos, technological strides march forward. Innovations emerge, promising faster, more scalable networks, novel applications, and a glimpse of what's yet to come. Each advancement paints a new stroke in this evolving masterpiece, hinting at an unseen future.

The rise and fall—the very heartbeat of this narrative— embody the human spirit, pulsating with greed, fear, hope, and ambition. It's a symphony of emotions played out in digital realms, where every surge and plunge mark a chapter in a tale that transcends financial metrics—a story of our collective journey into the unknown.

And as the story unfolds, one thing remains certain—the saga of cryptocurrencies, twists and turns, will continue to captivate, surprise, and perhaps redefine the essence of value and trust in our world.

Yet, as swiftly as the market ascended, it came crashing down, leaving devastation in its wake. The disillusionment was palpable as the once-soaring prices plummeted, mirroring the descent of a rollercoaster at its peak. It was as if the very foundation of our financial aspirations had crumbled beneath our feet, leaving us grappling with a harsh reality.

In the aftermath of this dramatic fall, the prevailing sentiment mirrored that of a Ponzi scheme. The disbelief and dismay echoed across the community, leaving a bitter taste of regret and uncertainty. Dreams that had felt so tangible and within reach now seemed distant and intangible, akin to a cruel twist of fate.

For me, it wasn't just a financial blow but a profound emotional setback. It felt like a gut punch, a relentless assault on the dreams and hopes I had invested in this burgeoning market. It wasn't just about the numbers on a screen; it was about the aspirations, the sacrifices, and the relentless hope that this new frontier of finance had promised.

The feeling of being caught in the whirlwind of this rise and fall was overwhelming. It wasn't just a market crash but a crash of faith, a blow to the belief that I, too, could carve a path to financial independence in this evolving landscape.

As the dust settled, what remained was the resilience to stand up again, to learn from the chaos, and to recognize that amidst the turbulence, valuable lessons emerged. It was a pivotal moment that would shape my approach, my understanding, and ultimately, my success in the world of cryptocurrency.

As tension thickened within the clinic walls, it seemed like an unseen storm was brewing. My boss, a figure of authority and certainty, had leaped into the world of cryptocurrency, investing a considerable amount of her hard-earned money. We all knew about her foray into this digital realm; it was a topic whispered about during lunch breaks and lingered in the air like an unspoken concern.

Then, like a bolt from the blue, the market tumbled. The once-promising digital currencies she'd entrusted her funds to plummeted in value, sending shockwaves through the entire clinic. It wasn't just a financial nosedive but a seismic shift in our stability. The atmosphere grew tense, suffocating almost as uncertainty loomed over us.

I witnessed the stress etched on her face, lines of worry replacing the usual confidence. Her investments, which had promised so much, suddenly seemed as ephemeral as vapor. The weight of that realization lingered in every interaction and every decision made within those clinic walls.

The impact rippled beyond her desk. It was in the hesitant conversations, the cautious glances exchanged among colleagues, and the subdued tone that engulfed our workplace. We were a team accustomed to facing challenges head-on, but this was different—an invisible threat that had penetrated the core of our professional stability.

Every passing day felt like an eternity as we braced ourselves, unsure of the following market update. The foundation of trust in our boss's decisions trembled, reflected in the collective unease that shadowed our daily routines.

I found myself caught between sympathy and fear. Sympathy for her bold venture into the unknown, for the risks she'd taken in pursuit of potential gains. Fear, however, was a persistent companion, whispering of the volatility and uncertainty that seemed to govern this digital financial realm.

Amidst this turmoil, I grappled with my emotions, torn between loyalty and the instinct to safeguard my financial stability. Once a bastion of shared purpose and camaraderie, the clinic now felt like a vessel adrift in a turbulent sea of market fluctuations.

In these moments of collective apprehension, I realized the profound impact of financial decisions beyond balance sheets and ledgers. It was a lesson in vulnerability, in the fragility of our perceived stability, and a stark reminder that the allure of quick gains could carry unforeseen consequences.

As I opened the clinic door that morning, a sense of determination surged within me. I knew I had to take charge of my destiny. I chose to put in every ounce of effort, push myself beyond limits, and embrace a path less traveled. That day, I made a pivotal decision: to bid farewell to the familiar walls of the clinic.

With a heart full of hope and a mind brimming with aspirations, I embarked on a journey that demanded sacrifices. It meant extra work hours, exhausting days, and bidding farewell to the comfort of routine. The decision to part ways wasn't merely a career shift; it symbolized a leap of faith, a bold stride towards a future beyond the clinic's confines.

Pulling overtime became my mantra, my avenue to build something beyond the ordinary. Each extra hour was a brick laid in the foundation of my dreams. It wasn't just about the extra income but about fueling my ambition and gathering resources for a future I was determined to shape on my terms.

As I walked away from the clinic that day, it wasn't a farewell to a job but a hello to possibilities. It was a moment of liberation, a declaration of my intent to seize control of my destiny. The decision was daunting, but it was also liberating, empowering—a pivotal moment that set the stage for the remarkable journey ahead.

Leaving wasn't an end, just a change of scenery. Even as I walked away, a small voice kept urging me to dip my toes into the crypto waters. It was a nagging curiosity, a relentless whisper that refused to fade. So, despite the distance, I began to tiptoe into the cryptocurrency world.

Oddly enough, some of my earliest ventures into this realm occurred in the ICU amidst the bustle of pharmaceutical discussions among my coworkers. Their conversations often drifted toward traditional stocks, the rise and fall of markets, and the potential gains and losses. At first, it was just background noise, but gradually, those murmurs piqued my interest.

While I tended to patients or organized medications, snippets of financial chatter floated around me. They spoke of trends, market volatility, and the allure of digital currencies. My curiosity deepened. Slowly, I began diverting spare change into this enigmatic world that felt thrilling and elusive.

There, in the hospital's sterile corridors, as monitors beeped in rhythmic unison and the urgency of medical care persisted, I found myself navigating a different landscape. It was a realm of digital possibilities, where numbers danced, and algorithms dictated potential gains. My role as a caregiver intertwined with a newfound fascination for the financial realm, each moment at the hospital becoming an unexpected classroom for my nascent journey into crypto.

The contrast was stark—here I was, amid the life-and-death routines of a medical setting, while my mind wandered into the digital cosmos of investments and markets. In these moments of quiet juxtaposition, my fascination with crypto grew, fueled by a curiosity that refused to be contained.

Each conversation I overheard, each mention of stocks or market fluctuations, acted as a beacon, drawing me further into a realm that seemed distant yet oddly accessible. In the calm moments between patient check-ins, I found myself researching, learning, and dipping my toes into a world that held both mystery and promise.

So, while physically present in the heart of healthcare, my mind often roamed the labyrinth of cryptocurrencies, silently laying the groundwork for what would later become a defining chapter in my life.

I vividly recall the conversation, sitting among friends, sipping on steaming mugs of coffee. The topic of cryptocurrency surfaced, and I curiously asked for their thoughts. Their reaction? Laughter—a chorus of dismissive chuckles that echoed through the room. With a meager portfolio of around $2000 invested in various digital currencies at that time, I hesitantly divulged my position.

"You're throwing your money away," they collectively opined, the weight of their skepticism hanging heavy in the air. It was a moment that lingered—a room filled with laughter, doubt, and disbelief directed squarely at my budding interest in this unconventional financial landscape.

Their reaction stung, yet it fueled a determination within me. Their dismissal only strengthened my resolve to prove them wrong. Little did they know that a seemingly insignificant portfolio was the seed of a journey that would rewrite my financial narrative.

Their skepticism became the catalyst for my relentless pursuit of knowledge and understanding in the realm of cryptocurrency. It wasn't merely about defying their doubts; it became a personal quest to uncover the potential hidden within the enigmatic world of digital assets.

With each skeptical comment replaying in my mind like a persistent echo, I immersed myself in research, soaking up every detail about blockchain, market trends, and the underlying technology powering these digital currencies.

Every doubt they voiced only fueled my determination to comprehend this complex landscape, to decode its mysteries, and to find my footing amidst the chaos of the market.

Their laughter transformed into background noise, drowned out by my growing confidence and the clarity emerging from the chaotic world of cryptocurrencies. Little did they realize that their skepticism was the spark that ignited my unyielding passion and determination to carve a path to financial success in the most unconventional of places.

In hindsight, their laughter was the prelude to a journey of self-discovery and unwavering belief in the potential of an industry that, to many, remained an enigma. It was the moment when I resolved not just to prove them wrong but to prove to myself that even in the face of collective disbelief, determination could be the catalyst for unforeseen success.

That pivotal moment among friends, cloaked in skepticism and laughter, marked the beginning of a journey that would transform my life in ways I never imagined possible.

The room fell silent as their doubtful gazes met mine, their skepticism almost tangible. It was that look that conveyed their uncertainty and lack of belief in my aspirations. But I stood there, resolute, with an unwavering determination.

I remember it vividly, the weight of their doubts pressing against me. They couldn't see what I saw or feel the pulse of the market, the potential that lay dormant within the digital realms of cryptocurrency.

I held their gaze, each passing second an unspoken challenge. Their disbelief fueled the fire in my belly. They didn't understand the countless hours I'd spent poring over charts, analyzing trends, absorbing every piece of information available about this brave new world of finance.

One of these days, I said, steady and determined, I'm going to prove you all wrong. One of these days, I'll say I told you so.

At that moment, it wasn't just a declaration but a vow— an oath to myself. It was a promise that echoed the countless sacrifices, the sleepless nights, and the audacity to pursue something unconventional.

Their doubtful expressions lingered, etching into my memory. It was a pivotal moment, a line drawn between their skepticism and my unyielding belief. Little did they know, those words ignited a fire within me, propelling me forward on a path that would defy their expectations and rewrite my destiny.

CHAPTER FOUR

A NEW CHAPTER

As the years ticked by, I stared at the shattered remains of what I had painstakingly built. The investments I had poured my heart and soul into seemed to crumble before my very eyes. Doubt crept in, echoing the skeptical whispers that had lingered at the edges of my consciousness. Those voices who had scoffed at my unconventional choices gained volume, almost mocking my decisions.

At times, I couldn't help but entertain the thought that they were right. Perhaps this world, this intricate dance of digital currencies and market volatility, was not meant for someone like me—a woman from the heart of Kentucky with dreams more significant than the mountains that cradled my home.

The weight of uncertainty settled like an uninvited guest, casting shadows on the resilience that had fueled my journey thus far. Moments of hesitation seeped into my mind, tempting me to surrender to the chorus of naysayers. Their words echoed, painting a bleak portrait of failure. It became a constant battle between my unwavering determination and the gnawing tendrils of self-doubt.

Yet, amidst this turmoil, a flicker of defiance persisted— a reminder of the grit that had propelled me to venture into this unpredictable domain in the first place. I had weathered storms before and scaled hurdles that seemed impossible. This setback was just another chapter in my narrative—a chapter that demanded resilience and unwavering faith in my capabilities.

With each setback came a lesson—lessons etched in the trials and tribulations of the market. The price of knowledge, I realized, was not always paid in gains but often in losses—lessons that shaped me, molded my strategies, and fortified my resolve.

In the depths of that uncertainty, I knew then that this was not the end of my story. It was merely a pivotal moment, a turning point that demanded introspection, adaptation, and a renewed sense of determination. For sometimes, the most remarkable triumphs emerge from the ashes of apparent failure.

Sitting in the comfort of my home, the Appalachian twilight painting the room in hues of warmth, I nestled into the familiar embrace of my old, trusted couch. It was one of those quiet evenings when time seemed to stretch, and I decided to catch up with my son, who had ventured far from the hills of Kentucky.

As his face lit up the screen before me, his voice carried the echoes of distant lands. Hey, Mom, have you checked your crypto lately?" His question was so random and unexpected amidst our casual conversation that I couldn't help but chuckle softly before replying, No, not recently. Been caught up with the usual, you know?

Little did I realize that this seemingly ordinary query was about to spark a series of events that would change the course of my financial journey. It was a simple exchange, just a son reaching out to his mother. Yet, it planted a seed of curiosity in my mind, a curiosity that would grow into an obsession to understand the intricate world of cryptocurrency.

I didn't know it then, but that moment would mark the genesis of a path I never anticipated walking—a journey through the thrilling highs and nerve-wracking lows of the digital currency landscape.

The sheer randomness of my son's question and the nonchalant tone in which it was posed concealed the avalanche of possibilities waiting to unfold. It was as if fate had chosen that moment, in the quiet solitude of my living room, to nudge me into a previously foreign and unfamiliar realm.

That evening, little did I know that my response, a simple "no," would become the catalyst for a series of choices and decisions that would lead to unexpected triumphs and heart-stopping setbacks in the volatile world of crypto trading. But in that serene moment, I could only smile, unaware of the rollercoaster ride awaiting me in the world of digital currency.

As I hung up the phone, my mind swirled with emotions. The words exchanged in that conversation echoed in my ears, the significance of what had just transpired settling into my consciousness. With disbelief and excitement, I made my way to my computer, fingers trembling as I logged into the account that had become a silent witness to my journey. This journey had taken an unexpected turn, transforming mere numbers on a screen into life-changing digits.

The name "Ethos" stared back at me from the screen, a name I had first stumbled upon years ago when cryptocurrency was whispered about in obscure corners of the internet. Back then, it was a speculative investment, a leap of faith driven by curiosity and a gut feeling. Now, it had morphed into "Voyager," its value soaring from those early few cents to an astonishing peak, proudly flashing $12.47.

For a fleeting moment, time seemed to stand still. The realization hit me like a thunderbolt—I had turned a modest investment into a substantial sum, an unexpected windfall that could rewrite the script of my life. The numbers danced before my eyes, confirming the inconceivable: a total of $78,000. It felt surreal, almost too unbelievable to grasp.

My heart raced, a surge of adrenaline coursing through me. I had to share this with someone, and there was no better confidant than my son. Dialing his number, my voice trembled as I relayed the news, the words stumbling over each other in my rush to articulate the magnitude of this moment. His disbelief mirrored my own, but as reality sank in, we formed a silent agreement.

We both knew what needed to be done. It was time to materialize this digital fortune, to transform these virtual gains into tangible reality. Together, we deliberated, weighing the possibilities and the risks. In unison, we decided to cash out to seize this opportunity that had presented so unexpectedly.

In that pivotal moment, as I closed the chapter on this particular investment, I couldn't help but marvel at the unpredictability of life and the twists and turns that led me to this remarkable outcome. It was a reminder that sometimes, against all odds, a leap of faith can defy expectations, transforming what was once a humble investment into an unforeseen triumph.

It was a rollercoaster ride, watching that figure drop by $25,000 just a month later. A surge of mixed emotions washed over me—worry, surprise, and a tinge of anxiety. But in the world of cryptocurrency, unpredictability reigned supreme. I had to act swiftly.

My first mission: finding a crypto exchange. The path to success in this digital realm wasn't just about investments; it was about navigating the platforms and the exchanges and finding the right fit. After a thorough search, luck met us at Huntington Bank's doorstep. With my two sons by my side—my pillars of support throughout this wild venture—we ventured in, determined to make our mark in the crypto world.

The air was charged with anticipation as we opened that account, a gateway to endless possibilities. Transferring that hard-earned money into the account felt like placing a bet on the future—exciting, nerve-wracking, and exhilarating. Each click and confirmation held the weight of potential, the promise of a new chapter in our lives.

The thought of what lay ahead filled me with determination and apprehension. Would this be the turning point, the catalyst for a transformative journey, or a leap into the unknown? But one thing was sure: I was ready to dive headfirst into this fast-paced, ever-shifting world of crypto, armed with research, determination, and an unwavering spirit.

In those tense moments at the bank, I felt the weight of skepticism bearing down on me like a heavy shroud. Converting my hard-earned cryptocurrency into USD felt like tiptoeing through a maze fraught with unseen pitfalls. Each digit, each transaction code, held the potential to tip the delicate balance between success and the terrifying abyss of a lost transfer.

The bank's skepticism echoed the doubts that sometimes crept into my mind, whispering, "Could this be a scam?" It wasn't just a matter of moving numbers but a high-stakes game of precision and accuracy. A single misstep, one tiny deviation in the code, and the currency could vanish into the cryptic labyrinth of the digital world, forever beyond reach.

The fear wasn't just about the conversion itself but the fear of losing the fruits of my labor, the culmination of relentless research, calculated risks, and sleepless nights tracking market fluctuations. The sweat on my palms mirrored the anxiety within—knowing that a single mistake could shatter the dreams I'd meticulously built.

The bank's cautious eyes mirrored the doubts of those who couldn't grasp the enigmatic world of cryptocurrencies. They couldn't see beyond the complexities of these transactions; to them, it might have seemed like a gamble rather than a well-thought-out investment.

But for me, it was a testament to my determination, a culmination of my unwavering belief in the potential of this burgeoning digital landscape. It was about transcending the conventional norms of finance, diving headfirst into a realm where each move carried the weight of opportunity and risk.

As I navigated through the conversion process, I held my breath, watching each digit meticulously, triple-checking every entry. The intense relief flooding over me when the transaction finally cleared was indescribable. It wasn't just about the money; it was the triumph of overcoming the fear, the doubt, and the skepticism—proof that my journey through the volatile world of cryptocurrency was not in vain.

That moment at the bank wasn't just about converting currency; it was about proving to myself and the world that with meticulous attention to detail and unwavering determination, even the most daunting crypto-realm obstacles could be conquered.

As I watched the digital confirmation of my deposit flicker onto the screen, a rush of excitement mixed with a tinge of nerves coursed through me. This was a significant moment—a pivotal step in what I hoped would be a life-changing venture.

Turning to my sons, I could barely contain my enthusiasm. "Bring your bank information," I urged them, barely able to keep the grin from spreading across my face. They had no idea what was coming. With a sense of purpose and a confidence I hadn't felt in a while, I handed each of them a substantial sum—$20,000.

Their reactions were a mixture of surprise, disbelief, and perhaps a touch of skepticism. I almost saw the mental gears turning as they processed the unexpected windfall. "Mom, are you serious?" one of them asked, eyes wide with disbelief. "We were expecting maybe $5,000, tops!"

I chuckled at their disbelief, feeling a surge of pride at being able to provide for them in such a significant way. "Consider it an investment in your future," I told them, trying to convey the moment's weight. This wasn't just about money; it was about instilling in them the belief that seizing opportunities and taking calculated risks could lead to unexpected rewards.

Their stunned expressions slowly transformed into wide grins, and at that moment, I knew I had given them more than just a sum of money. I had taught them the power of belief, the courage to defy expectations, and the thrill of taking a chance when the odds seemed against you.

Little did they know, this was just the beginning of a journey that would surpass all our expectations, where I would teach them not just about finances but about resilience, determination, and the belief that greatness can emerge from the most unlikely places.

Growing up without a father figure was a defining aspect of our lives. It wasn't just my journey; it was about my sons, too. From the earliest memories, it was evident that our lives would be different. We didn't have that guiding presence, that paternal figure whose advice and support were taken for granted by many. But rather than letting it be a source of despair, I saw it as a challenge—a chance to pave a different path for us all.

I made a silent promise to myself and my sons: I would be the one to change our narrative. It became my mission to provide them with what we had missed—a sturdy foundation, a head starts in a world that often felt daunting and uncertain.

There was an innate desire to offer them opportunities, to create a better future that wasn't dictated by the absence of a father. It was my way of rewriting our story, turning a blank page into a tale of resilience and determination.

Investing in their future became my priority. Every decision I made and every sacrifice I endured was with their well-being in mind. I delved into uncharted territories, seeking ways to secure a better tomorrow for all of us.

Financial stability was just a part of it. It was about instilling values, nurturing dreams, and building security beyond material comforts. I wanted them to know that despite life's adversities, we had the power to carve our destinies.

It was a challenging road. There were sacrifices—late nights working extra shifts, moments of uncertainty, and occasions where doubts clouded my mind. But the thought of providing my siblings with a more vital starting point fueled my determination. I was determined not to let the absence of our father define us.

Through it all, I held on to the belief that our past didn't determine our future. And so, in the face of adversity, I forged ahead, striving to provide my siblings with the foundation they deserved, a stepping stone to a brighter, more promising tomorrow.

Getting to pay off my house was an incredible moment that filled me with a sense of security and accomplishment like never before. Picture this: the rugged beauty of the Appalachian Mountains forming the backdrop as I stood outside my home in Kentucky, the place I'd always known as my sanctuary.

The feeling of holding that final payment, knowing that my home was indeed mine—no bank, no creditor, no one could ever take it away. It was a moment of triumph, a testament to the hard work and determination that had driven me on this incredible journey through cryptocurrency.

I reminisce about the countless hours of overtime I'd put in, and the sacrifices made, all for this defining moment. The idea that my home, the heart of my existence, was now secure sparked a sense of freedom within me— freedom to dream bigger, take bolder steps, and embrace the opportunities ahead.

But beyond the material aspect, the emotional weight that lifted off my shoulders made this moment so profound. The peace of mind that came with owning my home outright—knowing that it was a foundation for not just me but also my dreams and aspirations. It validated every risk taken and every bold decision made in the volatile world of cryptocurrency.

As I closed the chapter on mortgage payments, I felt a surge of gratitude for the journey that had led me here. It wasn't just about financial stability but about carving out a space where my determination and hard work translated into a tangible, lasting asset—a place I could call my own, a symbol of resilience and perseverance against all odds. And in that moment, I stood there, looking at my home, feeling an overwhelming sense of pride and accomplishment that words can barely encapsulate.

With the weight of mortgage payments lifted off my shoulders, a newfound sense of freedom and possibility dawned upon me. I found myself contemplating new horizons, setting my sights on ventures beyond the confines of my once-burdensome financial obligations.

The security of owning my home outright ignited a fire, propelling me to explore further possibilities in the world of investments. It wasn't just about accumulating wealth anymore; it was about leveraging this stability to make calculated moves that could shape my future and, in turn, impact the lives of those around me.

As I delved deeper into the world of cryptocurrency, my ambitions expanded. I sought to diversify my investment portfolio, exploring avenues aligned with my newfound financial freedom. This wasn't merely about chasing profits but about strategic decisions and mindful investments that resonated with my vision for the future.

The journey wasn't without its challenges. With newfound resources came greater responsibilities—decisions carried heavier weight, and risks had more significant implications. I had to adapt, refine my strategies, and sometimes recalibrate my approach. The crypto market remained as dynamic and unpredictable as ever, demanding constant vigilance, research, and a balanced approach to risk-taking.

Beyond personal gain, I found a growing desire to share my knowledge and experiences. The newfound stability gave me a platform to mentor and guide individuals within my community who sought to navigate the complexities of cryptocurrency. Being able to offer insights and support to those eager to learn became an unexpected yet fulfilling part of my journey.

Yet, amidst these new ventures and expanded horizons, I remained rooted in the principles that had guided me from the beginning—perseverance, diligence, and a commitment to continuous learning. The financial security of owning my home was not just a destination but a stepping stone toward a future where my aspirations knew no bounds.

As I charted this new chapter of my life, I couldn't help but marvel at the transformative power of a single milestone. Paying off my house wasn't merely a financial feat; it was a catalyst for a broader vision of success that transcended monetary gains and aimed to leave a lasting impact on my own life and the world around me.

As I delved deeper into the dynamic realm of digital assets, I realized that the landscape was constantly in flux. What had worked in the past may not yield the same results in the ever-evolving crypto market. So, I adapted.

I began recalibrating my investment strategies, armed with knowledge gained from prior successes and the lessons learned from the challenges encountered along the way. It wasn't just about making gains anymore; it was about preserving and growing the wealth I'd worked so hard to accumulate.

Diversification emerged as a fundamental principle in my approach. While my initial success stemmed from a handful of bold investments, I understood the importance of spreading risk across a broader spectrum of assets. I meticulously researched and diversified my portfolio, balancing high-potential assets with more stable ones to cushion against market volatility.

However, this transition was challenging. With its rapid fluctuations and unpredictable trends, the crypto sphere posed new challenges. The emotional rollercoaster of seeing investments soar to new heights one day and plummet the next tested my financial acumen and emotional resilience.

The lessons I learned during this phase were invaluable. Patience became my ally as I navigated through periods of market dips and unforeseen fluctuations. I embraced a more analytical approach, constantly studying market trends, understanding technological advancements, and staying attuned to global events that impacted the crypto space.

But it wasn't just about crunching numbers and analyzing charts; it was about the people—the vibrant community that thrived within this sphere. Engaging with like-minded individuals, exchanging ideas, and learning from the collective wisdom of the crypto community became an integral part of my journey.

Amidst the complexities and uncertainties, one thing remained constant: the need to adapt and evolve. The payoff of my house was not just a destination but a stepping stone toward refining my strategies, learning from setbacks, and embracing a more nuanced approach to the ever-evolving world of cryptocurrency.

CHAPTER FIVE

EMPOWERMENT AND LEGACY

The lessons etched into my soul from this odyssey were beyond the mere arithmetic of profit and loss. Each digital coin I watched fluctuate on my screen was a pixel in a larger picture—a testament not only to the ever-shifting tides of the market but to the unwavering spirit that navigates them.

In those solitary moments, hunched over my computer amidst the luminescent glow of charts and data, I learned the value of perseverance. It wasn't just about the numbers, though they danced before me like cryptic poetry. It was the resilience forged through countless nights of research, through the labyrinth of white papers and market analyses.

Every rise and fall, every unexpected surge or sudden dip, gifted me with financial insight and a deeper understanding of the unpredictable rhythm of life itself. The market, akin to the wild Appalachian landscape I call home, taught me the art of adaptability, of swiftly adjusting sails when the winds of change swept through.

But beyond the spreadsheets and market trends, the most profound lesson was the unyielding strength found within. The belief that from the quiet corners of Kentucky, I could challenge the status quo of finance. It was a revelation that extended far beyond the glow of my screen—a belief that, armed with determination and an unquenchable thirst for knowledge, barriers could be shattered and stereotypes debunked.

The journey through cryptocurrency wasn't solely about amassing wealth; it was a transformative pilgrimage. No matter how modest, each victory stitched together a tapestry of resilience and self-discovery. It became a testimony to the sheer audacity of dreams and the immense power hidden within the folds of determination.

In this domain of digital currencies, the rewards transcended the material—the gains weren't merely financial; they were philosophical. The worth I discovered in my quest wasn't limited to numbers in a bank account; it was the richness of experience, the depth of knowledge, and the unwavering belief that, against all odds, greatness could be sculpted from sheer determination and audacity.

CRYPTO: FROM HILLS TO HOLDINGS

The invaluable currency I collected wasn't just Bitcoin or Ethereum; it was the priceless wisdom gleaned from every twist and turn of this riveting journey.

As the minutes ticked by, a friendly conversation began with a fellow patient, and the topic turned to the enigmatic realm of finance. With a subtle spark of interest, I shared bits of my experience navigating the digital currency landscape.

At first, it was just a casual chat, an exchange of anecdotes about the market's unpredictability and the thrill of investments. But as words spilled from my lips, a sense of amazement and curiosity lit up the faces around me. They hung onto every word, their eyes widening with each detail of my journey.

It was a peculiar moment—a mixture of surprise and awe painted across their expressions. Some whispered in hushed tones, while others regarded me with newfound respect. In that instant, the atmosphere shifted, and I found myself unwittingly cast in the spotlight.

People began asking questions, seeking advice and insights, treating me like I held the keys to financial wisdom. It was surreal. The "financial guru" title suddenly clung to me like an unexpected cloak. I am a small-town individual from the Appalachian hills, now seen as a beacon of financial knowledge.

But deep down, amidst the whispered conversations and newfound admiration, I couldn't help but feel the weight of expectation settling on my shoulders. The pressure to live up to this accidental pedestal, to dispense sage advice, and to maintain the aura of expertise became an unforeseen challenge.

I smiled and nodded, trying to impart what little wisdom I had garnered through my journey. Yet, at that moment, I realized that my story, while remarkable, was not about being a financial oracle—it was about the resilience to venture into the unknown and make it despite the odds.

With a sly grin, I couldn't help but shoot a triumphant glance at my friends from the pharmacy. For years, they'd nodded politely while I fervently discussed the potential of cryptocurrency. Back then, my enthusiasm was met with skeptical smiles and the occasional eye roll. Yet, as I stood there, witnessing the soaring numbers on my digital wallet, a part of me wanted to exclaim, "I told you so!"

The memory took me back to our countless conversations over coffee and late-night dinners. I'd passionately explained blockchain technology's decentralized nature and its transformative power. My friends, absorbed in the traditional financial world, had their reservations. They'd warned me about the volatility, the risks, and the lack of regulatory backing. And truth be told, they weren't entirely wrong.

The journey into the crypto realm was a rollercoaster of adrenaline-fueled highs and nerve-wracking plunges. But amidst the market's wild fluctuations, I persisted. Late nights turned into early mornings as I meticulously studied whitepapers, analyzed market trends and tracked the whispers of promising altcoins. It was a gamble that demanded not just financial investment but a mental fortitude to weather the storms.

Then came that pivotal moment, a blink-and-you'll-miss-it surge in the value of a lesser-known token I'd dared to invest in. The disbelief and awe were palpable as my wallet inflated, reflecting gains that seemed implausible in the conventional financial sphere. And in that instance, as I stood face-to-face with the tangible fruits of my risk-taking, a part of me wanted to share the victory with those who'd doubted me.

But rather than gloat, I held back, letting the numbers speak for themselves. There was a silent satisfaction in knowing that while their skepticism had been warranted, my belief in the potential of this nascent technology had paid off. It was a lesson in resilience, in believing in something many deemed uncertain—a lesson that extended far beyond the numbers on a screen.

As I turned away, I couldn't help but feel a sense of validation, not just for my gains but for the countless hours of research, the sleepless nights, and the unwavering belief in a vision that others found hard to grasp.

Walking through the streets of my town, I became a magnet for questions about cryptocurrency. Everyone wanted advice, a quick tip leading them to their financial breakthrough. And my response, almost like a reflex, became a constant refrain: "Do your own research."

I'd pause, meeting their eager gazes with a hint of caution. Any money you put in, consider it already in motion. You can't afford to obsess over it, to let every market fluctuation dictate your emotions. It wasn't just advice but a mantra I lived by; a philosophy carved from my own experiences in the whirlwind of digital currencies.

But behind those succinct lines lay a wealth of hard-earned lessons. I'd learned that diving into the crypto realm demanded more than just an initial investment; it demanded a commitment to understanding the dynamics, the trends, and the underlying technology. It was a world where fortunes fluctuated like the erratic beat of a drum and where anxiety could become a constant companion if you let it.

Those words, do your own research, encapsulated a journey filled with sleepless nights poring over whitepapers, scrutinizing market charts until they blurred, and engaging in discussions that felt like a maze of conflicting opinions. I'd discovered that the most valuable asset in this realm wasn't just money but knowledge—the ability to discern, sift through the noise, and make informed decisions.

So, amidst the constant inquiries and the hopeful eyes seeking a shortcut to success, my response held a dual purpose: to impart wisdom while instilling a sense of responsibility. It wasn't about handing out fish; it was about teaching the art of fishing in these turbulent digital waters.

And yet, in that bustling exchange of words on the streets, I couldn't convey the total weight of the journey behind those simple phrases. The countless moments of uncertainty, the thrill of a successful investment, and the resilience built from weathering market storms—they were the silent companions to that advice.

Each time I repeated those words, it was a reminder to myself as much as it was guidance for others. It was a testament to the unyielding belief that, in the end, it was the personal understanding and conviction born from research and experience that paved the path to success in the ever-evolving world of cryptocurrency.

It was an unexpected whirlwind; those fifteen minutes felt like a lifetime. The sudden surge of attention and the spotlight thrust upon me was surreal. As I basked in the glow of this newfound attention, reminiscing about my journey from the hills of Kentucky to this exhilarating moment, I couldn't help but ponder my past at the clinic.

Leaving that place of employment was a pivotal decision—a leap of faith, some would say. Looking back, I wonder if they knew what they had let slip through their fingers. Was it luck that paved my path? Partly, perhaps. But diligence, determination, and an unyielding hunger to carve my destiny played a far more significant role.

The clinic was a chapter of my life that taught me resilience in the face of challenges. I remember the long hours, the dedication poured into every task, and the persistence that became my second nature. And yet, when the time came to bid farewell, a sense of ambiguity lingered. Did they know the potential that lay within their grasp, the potential that I now carried forward into the world of cryptocurrencies?

In those fifteen minutes of fame, amidst the interviews and the sudden recognition, I couldn't help but smile at the irony of it all. Unaware of the force they had in their midst, the clinic unknowingly became a stepping stone for what was to come. Was I lucky? Undoubtedly. But luck alone didn't craft my story. It was a blend of perseverance, self-belief, and an unshakable resolve to carve a path uniquely mine."

CHAPTER SIX

THE RIPPLE EFFECTS

B ecoming involved in cryptocurrency wasn't just about making money but changing my financial trajectory entirely. With every successful investment, my confidence grew, propelling me to explore other avenues for financial growth.

As the world slowly emerged from the grip of the pandemic, an opportunity presented itself—one that I couldn't ignore. I made a decision that would shape my financial landscape even further: becoming a travel respiratory therapist. It wasn't just a job but a gateway to a stream of income that surpassed all my expectations.

In the wake of COVID-19, healthcare demand surged, especially for specialized roles like respiratory therapists. This sudden demand created a lucrative market for those willing to travel and lend their expertise where needed most. I seized this chance, not just for the financial rewards but also for the chance to contribute meaningfully during those challenging times.

The pay was beyond what I had ever imagined. It wasn't just about the numbers on a paycheck but about the opportunities it afforded me. With this newfound income, I made a bold move that I had only dreamed of—investing in real estate.

I chose a college town bustling with life and potential. It felt like the perfect environment to dive into the world of property investment. Purchasing not just one but two duplexes became a reality. These weren't just buildings; they were my foothold in real estate, a tangible asset I could see and touch.

The decision to rent them out wasn't solely about generating passive income—it was about creating a legacy and securing a stable future for myself and those around me. It was about leveraging the opportunities that life had presented me with, a testament to the belief that hard work, determination, and strategic financial decisions could shape a future far beyond my wildest dreams.

Every step in this journey was a testament to the power of taking risks, learning from experiences, and channeling newfound success into opportunities that perpetuated growth. It wasn't just about the money but the doors that opened when I dared to believe in my potential.

Venturing into the world of cryptocurrency wasn't just about financial gains for me; it became a testament to breaking barriers and proving that even a woman from the Appalachian Mountains could make waves in a fast-paced, tech-driven industry. Cryptocurrency opened doors I never imagined stepping through—a world where innovation and opportunity collided.

I remember the skepticism and raised eyebrows when I first mentioned my interest in digital currencies. 'A female from the hills dabbling in crypto?' they'd say. But that skepticism fueled my determination. It wasn't just about making profits; it was about shattering misconceptions and inspiring others of my age, from my community, and beyond.

Every success story has its roots in belief and perseverance. I wanted to be that living proof—a testament to the idea that anything is achievable with unwavering faith and persistence. My journey wasn't just about making money; it was about showing that even those from the most unlikely places could thrive in finance.

I learned invaluable lessons through the crypto market's peaks and valleys. The rollercoaster of emotions became my teacher, from the thrill of monumental gains to the daunting challenges of navigating volatility. It wasn't just about the numbers but the resilience and adaptability I developed with every trade and decision.

As I trod this path, I became an influencer—not in the conventional sense, but as someone who ignited hope and belief. I became a voice telling others that barriers are mere illusions and that age, gender, or geographic location shouldn't dictate one's potential. I wanted people to see that embracing the unknown, taking calculated risks, and having faith could lead to extraordinary outcomes.

Through crypto, I didn't just invest in digital currencies; I invested in the idea that anyone, regardless of background, could carve their destiny. The doors I opened weren't just for myself; they were to usher in possibilities for those who dared to dream beyond their circumstances.

Uncertainty shrouded my every step in the vast expanse of the Appalachian Mountains. I hailed from the heart of Kentucky, where dreams often felt like fleeting whispers against the rugged terrain. Financial stability was a luxury, a distant shimmer on the horizon I yearned to grasp.

Yet, amidst the echoes of doubt, an ember of determination burned within me. I toiled tirelessly, pouring my sweat into overtime work, each drop a testament to my unyielding resolve. The paychecks were hard-earned, but hope flickered alive within those earnings—the hope for a future less burdened by the constraints of financial insecurity.

Then came the moment—a serendipitous encounter with the enigmatic realm of cryptocurrency. It was as if the universe had unveiled its secrets, whispering promises of opportunity. With hesitance trembling in my heart, I dared to delve deeper, to educate myself about this digital frontier that seemed worlds away from the Appalachian landscape.

Armed with grit and a genuine hunger for change, I navigated through the labyrinth of information, voraciously consuming every ounce of knowledge I could grasp. Nights bled into days as I studied the market, deciphering the cryptic language of trends and charts, an odyssey into a previously unknown world.

With trepidation, I made my first investments—an echo of uncertainty lingering in each decision. But as days turned to weeks and weeks to months, the timid whispers of doubt transformed into jubilant cheers of triumph. The initial couple thousand dollars invested became a beacon of hope—a staggering $78,000 testament to resilience and unwavering determination.

The newfound financial prowess bestowed upon me an ability I never dreamed possible—to aid my family, alleviate their burdens, and rewrite our collective future narrative. The uncertainty that once loomed like a specter in the backdrop of our lives began to dissipate, replaced by the burgeoning possibility of a brighter tomorrow.

In those moments of transformation, as I stood at the intersection of my past struggles and newfound triumphs, I realized the profound truth: amidst the uncertainty, within the folds of relentless perseverance, lay the power to shape our destinies.

My journey from the hills of Kentucky to the world of cryptocurrency wasn't just about financial gain; it was a testament to the resilience of the human spirit, a symphony composed of setbacks, education, risk, and, ultimately, the triumphant crescendo of success against all odds.

In closing, my journey through the unpredictable landscape of cryptocurrency taught me invaluable lessons that transcend the pursuit of financial gain. It became a canvas upon which resilience, patience, and faith painted their profound truths.

I discovered resilience is not merely the ability to endure adversity but to thrive despite it. The unwavering spirit refuses to be shackled by doubts or setbacks, forging ahead even when the path seems obscured by shadows.

Patience, a virtue often overlooked in the frenzy of modern life, proved to be the silent orchestrator of my success. It's the art of waiting without losing hope and nurturing dreams while navigating through the ebb and flow of life's uncertainties.

Faith, a beacon that illuminated my darkest hours, wasn't just in the capricious world of cryptocurrency but in my capabilities, the relentless pursuit of knowledge, and the unwavering belief that even the most unlikely dreams can materialize with dedication and perseverance.

My story is not merely a tale of financial triumph; it's a testament to the dormant possibilities within each of us. It's a reminder that amid the tumultuous seas of life, anchored in the depths of our souls, lie the unwavering virtues of resilience, patience, and faith—virtues that can weather storms, defy expectations, and sculpt futures beyond imagination.

As you close this book, may you carry with you the echoes of my journey as a testament to the power within. May it serve as a reminder that no dream is too audacious, no goal too distant, and no challenge too formidable when met with resilience, patience, and unyielding faith.

For within the heart of every obstacle lies an opportunity; within the chaos resides the seed of creation, and within each of us, a reservoir of strength is waiting to be unleashed upon the canvas of our extraordinary lives. Embrace it, nurture it, and let the symphony of your journey echo across the landscapes of possibility.

With gratitude for sharing my story,

PAMELA FUGATE

www.ingramcontent.com/pod-product-compliance
Lightning Source LLC
Chambersburg PA
CBHW062350290526
45794CB00005B/2162